My Gift of
<u>Difference</u>
7 Steps to Embracing Your Learning Difference

Jordan Ashley Greene

ISBN-10: 1519649274
ISBN-13: 978-1519649270

DEDICATION

This book is dedicated to my parents and my brother CJ for helping me see that I am smart, gifted and talented; my grandparents Willie and Denise Jordan; and Callie Pringle, for believing in me, my extended family who loves me unconditionally, and all kids around the world who have the "Gift of Difference."

A special thanks to my dad, Carlton Greene, who patiently helps me get through my homework, and a special thanks to my mom, Jil Greene, who patiently worked with me on this project to help me find my voice.

I also want to thank my little cousins. McKenzie Love and Morgan Rose, for inspiring me to follow my dreams.

CONTENTS

1

THE MOMENT

I remember watching an old episode of "The Cosby Show." The Cosby show is about the life of a family with two parents, four daughters and a son. The son's name was Theo, and he was known to struggle sometimes in school.

One day he was upset because after studying very hard, he scored a low grade on a test. Theo was given an opportunity to revise and re-write the test but even then, he still received a poor grade. He was discouraged and frustrated because it appeared that no matter how hard he studied, he struggled to get a good grade on the test.

His parents had a meeting with his teacher, and based on the type of challenges he was having, she suggested he get tested for dyslexia.

Dyslexia is a learning disability which causes a person not be able to recognize words that are misspelled as easily as a someone who does not have it. Also, people with dyslexia have challenges reading. They might change words around or add words where they shouldn't be. This is an example of what it looks like for some readers with dyslexia.

Example of Dyslexia:

> The ord sare n otsp aced cor rect ly.
>
> We spell wrds xatle az tha snd to us. Sometimesalltheletters arepushedtogether.

Theo was relieved to finally figure out what was going on with him. As I watched this TV show, I began to think about some things I had been experiencing in school. At that moment, I thought I knew. I turned to my mom and said, "Mom, maybe I have dyslexia or a Learning Difference." I would discover a year later, that I didn't have Dyslexia. I had ADD, which is also a Learning Difference.

LEARNING DIFFERENCES

In simple terms, a learning difference results from a difference in the way a person's brain is "wired." Kids with learning differences are as smart as their peers. However, they may have trouble reading, writing, spelling, remembering or organizing information if left to figure things out by themselves.

There are 13 different types of learning differences that currently exist. Some kids learn better by hearing things; this is an auditory learning style. Some kids learn better using their hands so they need a manipulative approach, while others may require visual connection to grasp what is being taught.

When you have a learning difference, it's important to figure out the technique that suits you best. It's just a difference, it's not a disadvantage.

3

ADHD & ADD

ADHD stands for Attention Deficit Hyperactive Disorder. This condition sometimes makes it difficult to stay focused, or pay attention for long periods of time. For some kids, it can mean they have so much energy trapped inside of them it's hard to sit still. ADHD is a real condition. It can impact academic performance, and affect how well kids get along with others.

7

ADHD is becoming more and more common.

Doctors can find out if kids have it as early as 5

years old, but it's common not to discover it in girls

until fifth or sixth grade.

There is also a condition called ADD or

Attention Deficit Disorder. The kids in this group

have trouble focusing, or are considered to be

inattentive.

These are some of the things kids with ADD struggle with:

- **being easily distracted**
- **often forgetful, even in daily activities**
- **have trouble paying close attention to details in school, making careless mistakes**
- **sometimes ignoring a teacher, even when spoken to directly**
- **following instructions, failing to finish schoolwork or chores**
- **have trouble with organization and loses important things needed for homework**
- **dislikes and avoids tasks that require long periods of mental effort, such as homework**

Guess what? Adults can have ADHD too!!

Look at the list of famous people who have either ADHD, ADD or a similar Learning Difference.

NAME	TITLE
Whoopi Goldberg	Actress/Talk Show Host
Alexander Graham Bell	Scientist/Inventor
Thomas Edison	Inventor
Albert Einstein	Physicist/Scientist
Leonardo Da Vinci	Artist
Pablo Picasso	Artist
Muhammad Ali	Boxer
Henry Ford	Business Man/Founder of Ford Motor Company
William Hewlett	Engineer/Co-Founder of Hewlett-Packard Computer Company
Paul Orfalea	Founder of Kinkos
Solange Knowles	Singer/Model
Justin Timberlake	Singer/Actor
Michael Phelps	Olympic Swimmer

4

THE 5TH GRADE FIGHT

I was in fifth grade when I discovered I had ADD. As I looked back over the last few years in school, I began to notice some things about myself. I had trouble spelling words (sometimes I would reverse letters, or leave some out), and I began to have trouble with math. For some reason, I couldn't get the numbers straight, or I couldn't remember rules I had learned to apply to math problems, which began to show in my grades. I remember being placed in certain math groups for kids who were on the same level as I was. I remember wanting to be in a different group, a higher group. I felt a little down, because I felt like everybody else understood what was going on except me.

By the time I got to 5th grade, I felt like it had all fallen apart. My family and I had just moved to a new city, which meant a new school. I felt the pressure of being the new girl, having left my old friends, I now had to make new ones. In addition to the transition, my school work seemed to get more difficult. I would sit in class and try my best to pay attention but, I couldn't remember everything that was taught, I couldn't understand everything. I tried harder and harder and nothing changed. There were many tear-filled nights trying to get through homework with my parents help.

Nights like these left me feeling frustrated, discouraged, and not smart. I was sad and often angry because my parents didn't understand what I was going through, and I couldn't explain it to them so they could help me. It didn't seem like anybody could.

I would go in my room sometimes and cry myself to sleep. Other times, I would listen to music, write in my journal, or draw pictures to express what I was feeling. Sometimes I would go outside and hit the tree in the backyard just to let out my frustration. My mom and dad would hug me while I cried, but none of us knew what to do.

5

THE LEARNING DOCTOR

One day my Mom told me she was taking me to see "The Learning Doctor." I now know it was a psychologist. A psychologist is a doctor who specializes in helping kids and parents find out what's going in their brain.

I didn't quite know what to expect when I arrived for the appointment. My "Learning Doctor" was a very tall, with big hands. He had a nice smile, and soft voice which made me relax a little. The lobby, which had a calming beige color, was as quiet as a library and there were no other patients at that time.

It seemed like I was in the office forever. The doctor gave me lots of tests (or what doctors call assessments) that measured how my brain works, how fast it understands information, how well I remember things, how well I could put things in proper order, and how well I could pay attention for long periods of time. As I took the different tests, I tried to do my best and often wondered if my mom was still waiting in the lobby.

When I completed the tests, Mom and the doctor talked privately. He told her he had good news. The tests showed that I am extremely intelligent and that I did very well on the majority of the tests. I actually scored above grade level in several areas.

However, there were 3 areas that I had trouble with; the test that measured how well **I paid attention**, how well **I remembered** (my working memory) and how well **I recognized letters or number that were reversed** (which explains my trouble in math). The doctor also discovered **I needed glasses**. There were times when I would read and the words seemed to blur a little; or I would reverse the letters.

This is an example of what it looks like sometimes when I read:

A chlid taht sees lkie tihs can psas a vsioin screeinng

A child that sees like this can pass a vision screening..

After another set of tests and evaluations, I was diagnosed with ADD. After finding out I had ADD, I was relieved in a way. It meant I was smart, but that I just learned differently.

6

THE CURE

I began to do my own research on Google and YouTube to get a better understanding of ADD. I found out that there are different ways kids and parents deal with it.

How you deal with ADD, or other Leaning

Differences is called a treatment plan. The treatment plan you get depends on how ADD is affecting you. Everyone who has ADD or a Learning Difference is affected differently. As I said before, some kids might be hyperactive. They can't sit still in class, and might even be seen as having a behavioral problem.

Some kids may zone out, have trouble paying attention, or get distracted very easily. This could cause them to miss important information about their lessons or assignments.

Some kids may feel like their brain is overloaded, so they may understand things a lot slower than the rest of the class, or forget things they have known for a long time. Things that most people know go in order, like months of the year, kids with ADD might have to think about, or even forget.

MY PLAN

My parents started working with my teachers to put together a treatment plan that would help me in school. A part of my treatment plan included something called 'accommodations'. This is a system your teacher puts in place to help you learn in the way that suits you best.

On my plan, the teachers give me extra time on tests, will rewrite the instructions if I am confused or don't understand, and I also have a math tutor.

Test Instructions without Accommodations:

Please follow directions below:

Please read the following paragraph and circle the subject, underline each verb phrase, and draw a second line under all helping verbs.

Test Instructions with Accommodations:

Please follow directions below:

1) Please read the paragraph carefully
2) **Circle** the **Subject ONCE**
3) **Underline the Verb Phrase ONCE**
4) **Underline the Helping Verbs TWICE**
5) **Check each sentence against this checklist**

Even after you get a plan, you may have to make changes as you learn more about how you learn best.

Some parents and doctors believe that

medication should be included in the treatment plan. They believe medicine can help the brain slow down or speed up, which helps the kid to be more focused.

I don't know a lot about that because medicine isn't part of my plan, but it is for a lot of kids.

HERE IS A LIST OF COMMON ACCOMMODATIONS THAT ARE GIVEN TO KIDS WITH LEARNING DIFFERENCES:

1) Sit in front of the class near the teacher

2) Given more time to take tests

3) Have the test read out loud

4) Have the test taken at different times

5) Using recording devices during class

6) Student gets a Buddy to help with Homework getting written down

7) Medication

8) Tutor

IT'S A DIFFERENCE, NOT A DISADVANTAGE

In the beginning when I didn't know I had ADD, it was stressful and frustrating not knowing what was wrong. Sometimes I felt embarrassed, and alone. Now that I know, I still get frustrated on some days but now I understand myself and what's happening. God made me this way, and I am still great, I just learn differently, and sometimes have to do things at a different pace, or in a different way.

I am a happy 6th grade student. I am smart, inspirational, talented, creative and athletic. My friends describe me as fun, fair and a peace maker (that's funny). My coach describes me as tough and a competitive leader. My teachers describe me as pleasant, kind, and hardworking.

My family describes me as beautiful, witty, creative, funny, crafty, intelligent, caring, sensitive, loving, family-oriented, vision driven, artistic, curious, awesome, sweet, articulate, a student of history, and an African American princess.

These are beautiful words that describe me. They make me smile and feel good about myself. I have talents that help me with my creativity, make me great at public speaking, and help me compete athletically Another word that describes me is…<u>ADD</u>….AND THAT'S OK!

I embrace my Gift of Difference.

There is still a lot to learn about ADD/ADHD, and other learning differences. I think that experts, doctors and parents are still trying to figure out some things too.

I want to encourage any kid who might be like me. Maybe you have ADD, dyslexia, or another learning difference. You will have some days when you feel discouraged or frustrated because maybe you didn't do well on a test, or report card.

Remember, you can't compare yourself to others. I realize I feel bad when I compare myself to someone else. Just do your best, stick to your plan, and say good things to yourself.

Always remember that the Learning Difference, is not who you are, and it's only <u>ONE</u> part of your life.

8

SELF ESTEEM

I learned from different Women's Empowerment conferences with my Mom, that good self-esteem helps you see yourself in a positive light. The better your self-esteem, the more confidence you have. The more confidence you have the better you are. I focus on things that make me feel good and build my confidence.

For example:

When I speak at a Girl's Youth Conference I feel **<u>Pumped Up!</u>**
When I run track I feel **<u>Like a Winner!</u>**
When I draw or paint I feel **Creative!**

Now it's your turn! Name 3 things you are good at, or love to do, and complete below:

When I_____ I feel_____

When I_____ I feel_____

When I_____ I feel_____

9

POWER WORDS

There are a lot of ways to improve your self-esteem.

One way is to focus on positive words that describe

you. I call these my **Power words**.

Power words build you up and remind you of your good traits. I encourage you to make it a habit to use Power words to build yourself up.

My mom says it takes about 30 days to make a habit. Get your family and friends to help you out, by asking them to send you positive words that describe you. Once you have 30, use the worksheet on the next page.

I will share my Power words and steps I have used to help me embrace my Learning Difference. I believe it can help you too!

These are some of the words that my family and friends use to describe me:

I would like to share some tips that have helped me cope with my learning difference.

10

7 STEPS TO EMBRACING YOUR GIFT OF DIFFERENCE

1. Get in the Know

2. Get the Right View on You

3. Get Your Feelings Out

4. Get Help

5. Get Good at Being You

6. Get a Good Attitude

7. Get Busy with What You Love to Do

1

Get in the Know

Do your own research, and get a good understanding of your learning difference.

Get the Right View

See yourself as talented and amazing! You may learn differently, and still be star!

3

Get Your Feelings Out

Don't wear a mask. Be honest about your feelings, and talk them out with someone you trust.

Use the Feelings Face Journal in the back of the book to help with this.

4

Get Help

Having a learning difference is more than any kid can handle alone.

Make sure you let your parents and teachers know what your needs are.

5

Get Good @ Being You

You are awesome because God made you that way! Don't compare yourself to friends or family.

There is something special about you. Embrace it.

Get A Good Attitude

Choose your 'tude! Make a decision to see things in a positive light, no matter how hard things may seem. They will always get better.

I am good at public speaking, sports and art. I find a way to do these things all of the time.

It increases my confidence, and helps me feel good about myself.

1. Ask your family and friends to send a list of positive words that describe you. Your goal is to get 30 words.

2. Write the words on the Power Words list sheet.

3. Write 1 Power Word on the 30 Day Challenge Page per day.

4. Circle the Feely Face that describes how you feel on that day.

5. Discuss it with your Parent, Counselor or Teacher every day.

All kids should feel powerful. It doesn't matter what their learning style is.

I have ADD, but it doesn't have me, because I am…POWERFUL!

ADD.. Awesome, Dynamic, and Determined!

POWER WORDS LIST

WRITE THE 30 POWER WORDS FROM YOUR FAMILY AND FRIENDS BELOW.

1	
2	
3	
4	
5	
6	
7	
8	
9	
10	
11	
12	
13	
14	
15	

16	
17	
18	
19	
20	
21	
22	
23	
24	
25	
26	
27	
28	
29	
30	

30 DAY POWER WORD CHALLENGE

Fill in your Power Word below.

Circle the Feely Face that describes your mood for the day.

DAY	POWER WORD	FEELY FACES
EX:	*Creative*	HAPPY DETERMINED SAD FRUSTRATED
1		HAPPY DETERMINED SAD FRUSTRATED
2		HAPPY DETERMINED SAD FRUSTRATED
3		HAPPY DETERMINED SAD FRUSTRATED
4		HAPPY DETERMINED SAD FRUSTRATED
5		HAPPY DETERMINED SAD FRUSTRATED
6		HAPPY DETERMINED SAD FRUSTRATED
7		HAPPY DETERMINED SAD FRUSTRATED
8		HAPPY DETERMINED SAD FRUSTRATED
9		HAPPY DETERMINED SAD FRUSTRATED
10		HAPPY DETERMINED SAD FRUSTRATED

49

Fill in your Power Word below.

Circle the Feely Face that describes your mood for the day.

DAY	POWER WORD	FEELY FACES
EX:	*Creative*	HAPPY DETERMINED SAD FRUSTRATED
11		HAPPY DETERMINED SAD FRUSTRATED
12		HAPPY DETERMINED SAD FRUSTRATED
13		HAPPY DETERMINED SAD FRUSTRATED
14		HAPPY DETERMINED SAD FRUSTRATED
15		HAPPY DETERMINED SAD FRUSTRATED
16		HAPPY DETERMINED SAD FRUSTRATED
17		HAPPY DETERMINED SAD FRUSTRATED
18		HAPPY DETERMINED SAD FRUSTRATED
19		HAPPY DETERMINED SAD FRUSTRATED
20		HAPPY DETERMINED SAD FRUSTRATED

My Gift of Difference

Fill in your Power Word below.

Circle the Feely Face that describes your mood for the day.

DAY	POWER WORD	FEELY FACES			
EX:	Creative	HAPPY	DETERMINED	SAD	FRUSTRATED
21		HAPPY	DETERMINED	SAD	FRUSTRATED
22		HAPPY	DETERMINED	SAD	FRUSTRATED
23		HAPPY	DETERMINED	SAD	FRUSTRATED
24		HAPPY	DETERMINED	SAD	FRUSTRATED
25		HAPPY	DETERMINED	SAD	FRUSTRATED
26		HAPPY	DETERMINED	SAD	FRUSTRATED
27		HAPPY	DETERMINED	SAD	FRUSTRATED
28		HAPPY	DETERMINED	SAD	FRUSTRATED
29		HAPPY	DETERMINED	SAD	FRUSTRATED
30		HAPPY	DETERMINED	SAD	FRUSTRATED

51

AWESOME!!

You have completed the 30 Day Power Word Challenge.

Every day you were reminded of how amazing you are and you had a chance to speak with your parents about your feelings.

As you continue to learn more about your learning difference, here is a list of great websites that have helpful information.

LIST OF HELPFUL WEBSITES

www.ReadingRockets.org
www.Kidshealth.org
www.Inspiration.com
www.Donjohnston.com
www.Nuance.com/naturallyspeaking
www.Chadd.org
www.Ldonline.org

THE AUTHOR

Jordan Ashley Greene is a 12 year old 6th grade student, who embraces her gift of difference.

Her desire is to help other kids overcome some of the discouraging feelings that may come with having a learning difference. She wants to remind the world…

that kids with learning differences are gifted….they just see the world differently.

To contact Jordan for speaking engagements, workshops, and youth conferences please contact: Jil Greene at jil.greene@gmail.com.

45341846R00034

Made in the USA
Middletown, DE
01 July 2017